# MY BOOK OF
# Dogs
## and
# Puppies

**Senior Editor** Roohi Sehgal
**US Senior Editor** Shannon Beatty
**Editors** Kathleen Teece, Niharika Prabhakar
**US Editor** Mindy Fichter
**Senior Art Editors** Ann Cannings, Nidhi Mehra
**Project Art Editor** Nehal Verma
**Assistant Art Editor** Rushil Pradhan
**Illustrator** Bettina Myklebust Stovne
**Jacket Designer** Ann Cannings
**DTP Designers** Dheeraj Singh, Mohd Rizwan
**Senior Picture Researcher** Sakshi Saluja
**Production Editor** Abi Maxwell
**Production Controller** John Casey
**Managing Editors** Jonathan Melmoth,
Monica Saigal
**Managing Art Editors** Diane Peyton Jones,
Romi Chakraborty
**Delhi Creative Heads** Glenda Fernandes,
Malavika Talukder
**Deputy Art Director** Mabel Chan
**Publishing Director** Sarah Larter

**Consultant** Dr. Bruce Fogle

Content in this title was previously published in
*The Everything Book of Dogs and Puppies* (2018)

First American Edition, 2023
Published in the United States by DK Publishing
1745 Broadway, 20th Floor, New York, NY 10019

Copyright © 2023 Dorling Kindersley Limited
DK, a Division of Penguin Random House LLC
24 25 26 27 10 9 8 7 6 5
008–333835–Feb/23

A catalog record for this book
is available from the Library of Congress.
ISBN: 978-0-7440-7394-2

DK books are available at special discounts when
purchased in bulk for sales promotions, premiums,
fundraising, or educational use. For details, contact:
DK Publishing Special Markets,
1745 Broadway, 20th Floor, New York, NY 10019
SpecialSales@dk.com

Printed and bound in China

For the curious
**www.dk.com**

**MIX**
Paper | Supporting
responsible forestry
**FSC™ C018179**

This book was made with Forest
Stewardship Council™ certified paper—
one small step in DK's commitment to
a sustainable future. For more information
go to www.dk.com/our-green-pledge

# Contents

**4** Top to tail

**6** Coats and colors

**8** Bringing a dog home

**10** Pooch parlor

**12** Family life

**14** Puppy power

**16** Terriers

**18** Airedale Terrier

**19** Jack Russell Terrier

**20** West Highland White Terrier

**21** Yorkshire Terrier

**22** Scottish Terrier

**23** Border Terrier

**24** Senses

**26** Tail talk

**28** Hounds

**30** Norwegian Elkhound

**31** Miniature Dachshund

**32** Afghan Hound

**33** Greyhound

**34** Beagle

**35** Bloodhound

**36** Barks and yaps

38 Sporting dogs

40 Weimaraner

41 Golden Retriever

42 American Cocker Spaniel

43 English Springer Spaniel

44 Chesapeake Bay Retriever

45 Brittany

46 Italian Spinone

47 Blue Picardy Spaniel

48 Working dogs

50 Saint Bernard

51 Siberian Husky

52 Komondor

53 Bernese Mountain Dog

54 Briard

55 Boxer

56 Newfoundland

57 Great Dane

58 Dogs with jobs

60 Herding dogs

62 Pembroke Welsh Corgi

63 Old English Sheepdog

64 Border Collie

65 German Shepherd

66 Nonsporting dogs

68 Dalmatian

69 Poodle

70 Chow Chow

71 Shiba Inu

72 Toy dogs

74 Chinese Crested Dog

75 French Bulldog

76 Pekingese

77 Pug

78 Bichon Frise

79 Cavalier King Charles Spaniel

80 Doggie delights

82 Crossbreeds

84 Labradoodle

85 Chiweenie

86 Training

88 Playtime

90 All together

92 Glossary

94 Index

96 Acknowledgments

# Top to tail

All dogs belong to the canine group, which also includes wolves, foxes, and jackals. Dogs are known for their instincts to herd, hunt, and guard. Humans mostly keep them as pets, and they are companions for life.

A dog has 319 to 321 bones in its body—over 100 more than a human!

Mobile ears pick up sounds from different directions.

Big eyes give dogs sharp eyesight.

Dogs from places with colder climates tend to have longer coats.

Taste buds on a dog's tongue detect if food is good to eat.

## Features of a dog

There are many dog breeds all over the world. While they vary in shape, size, and color, their basic body structure is the same.

# Large and little

Dogs can be big, medium, or small. When standing on its back legs, a Great Dane can be taller than its owner! Even on the ground, this breed can be over 28–30 in (71–76 cm) high, making it the world's biggest dog. The Chihuahua can be just over 6 in (15 cm) tall, making it the world's smallest dog.

**Chihuahua**          **Great Dane**

# Wolves to dogs

All dogs are descended from wolves. People first tamed wolves to use them as hunters and guards. As modern dogs developed, they inherited many features and behaviors from their ancestors.

**Gray wolf**

### Howling
Dogs howl like wolves to send messages to other dogs. Some dogs also howl in response to music or strange sounds.

A tail helps with balance when running.

Most dogs have strong, muscular legs that are good for running.

Dogs sweat through their paws, and have claws for gripping.

### Body language
Like wolves, dogs use their body posture and tail position to communicate with each other, and also with humans.

### Smell and sight
Dogs have kept the strong sense of smell and sharp sight of their wolf ancestors. Some dog breeds have better eyesight, while others have a more powerful sense of smell.

# Coats and colors

Dog hair can be short, long, silky, or rough. Some dogs have two types of hair. Topcoat hairs are longer. They grow past shorter, undercoat hairs, which sit close to the skin.

## Color varieties

Dog coats can be various colors. Some breeds may have a single color coat or a combination of two colors. Others may have several color variations.

Boxer

Chow Chow

Giant Schnauzer

## Short

Dogs with this type of coat have short hair. These dogs are the easiest to groom. Breeds including the Boxer, Dalmatian, Greyhound, and Labrador Retriever have short coats.

## Double

Many breeds have a double coat. The topcoat is waterproof, while the undercoat is soft and short. Breeds including the Chow Chow have a very thick double coat to help protect them in cold weather.

## Wire-haired

Wire coats, also called broken coats, feel rough when touched. Most terriers including the Giant Schnauzer are wire-haired. This coat is perfect for activities such as digging, or racing through bushes.

 Liver or red

 Blue

 Dark brown or chocolate

 Black

 Gold, tan, or liver and white

 Black and white

 Black, tan, and white

 Liver and tan

 Blue and tan

 Black and tan

 Brindle

 Other varieties

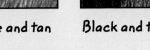 White, cream, or gray

Gold or fawn

Afghan Hound

Labradoodle

American Hairless Terrier

## Long straight

This type of hair helps dogs stay warm in cold temperatures. The Afghan Hound has the long, silky coat of its ancestors who lived in the mountains of Afghanistan—where it can get very cold.

## Curly

Some dogs, such as the Labradoodle, Bichon Frise, or Poodle, have thick, short curls. This kind of curly coat helps to protect a dog's skin in harsh conditions.

## Hairless

The American Hairless Terrier and the Chinese Crested Dog are two of the few dog breeds that are hairless. Such dogs may have no hair at all, or just a few strands on the head, feet, or tail.

# Bringing a dog home

There's a lot of excitement when a new furry friend is about to come home. There are also lots of tasks to be done in preparation for its arrival. Things that could be harmful for the dog need to be put away, and new owners should stock up on everything the dog needs.

Harnesses fit around the dog's body for the leash to be attached to.

**Harness**

Collars usually show the owner's phone number, and leashes can be attached to them—if owners are careful not to pull too hard.

**Leash and collar**

Two dog bowls are needed—one for food and one for water.

**Dog bowls**

**Grooming tools**

Grooming tools will help keep the dog's fur clean.

**Dog bed**

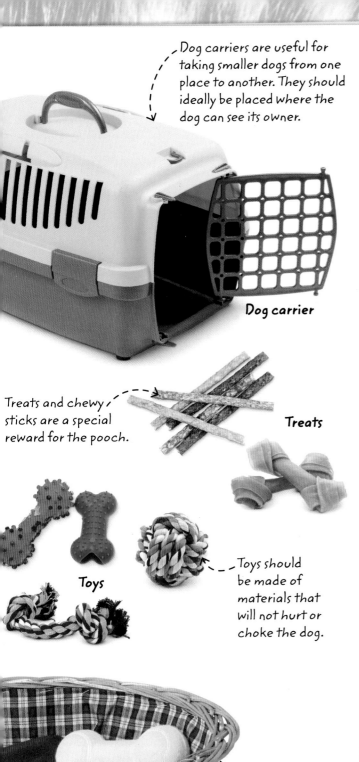

Dog carriers are useful for taking smaller dogs from one place to another. They should ideally be placed where the dog can see its owner.

**Dog carrier**

Treats and chewy sticks are a special reward for the pooch.

**Treats**

**Toys**

Toys should be made of materials that will not hurt or choke the dog.

Beds need to be comfy for the dog to lie in.

# A dog's day

Dogs like to eat, play, explore, walk, and sleep! They are happiest when they are with their owners. Here's what a usual doggie day looks like.

**Morning**
The dog is happy to wake up for walks. It loves to play with its owner. After a hearty breakfast, it's time to take a nap.

**Afternoon**
The pooch is ready for some more play. Then it will probably take a long drink of water. Gulp, gulp! The dog will now settle down on the floor or in its bed for a snooze.

**Evening**
After dinner, the dog is full of energy for some more fun games and exercise. One last walk outside, and then it's bedtime.

# Pooch parlor

There is never a bad hair day at the pooch parlor, where dog coats come in different colors, patterns, textures, and thicknesses. Regular grooming and bathing are good for the skin and coat, and also help prevent excessive hair shedding.

Dense coats need cleaning monthly, while short coats need it only a few times a year.

Dalmatian

## Short coat

This is the easiest coat to care for. A daily brush, and a good groom once a week using a hair dryer on low heat, is all that's needed to remove dead hairs. These dogs need a bath every three months.

Shih Tzu

## Long coat

Attention is needed for long coats. A daily groom prevents tangles. Big knots can be removed with a strong comb, and smaller tangles gotten rid of with a slicker brush.

## Essential supplies

Different grooming tools are right for different coat types. A fine-toothed comb works best for thin hair. A slicker brush is an all-purpose brush. Dog shampoo is used to clean the fur.

Hair clipper

Comb

Slicker brush

Dog scissors

Dog shampoo

# Hygiene

A dog's ears, nails, and teeth also need regular checks and care. But cleaning and trimming can be an unpleasant experience for dogs at first. Owners might use treats as rewards, and pet their pooches gently until they feel calm.

### Ear cleaning
A dog's ears should be examined at least once a month. If there is liquid seeping out, a bad smell, redness, or swelling, a trip to the vet is needed.

### Nail trimming
A dog's nails need regular trimming, which is best done by a vet or a trained groomer. Owners should also regularly inspect for any swelling or mats between the toes.

Fox Terrier

# Wiry or curly coats

These coats do not shed as much hair as other coats. The dogs' owners usually take them to an experienced dog groomer twice a year. Between visits, the coat can be trimmed with scissors or clippers to keep it in good condition.

### Teeth cleaning
Moist, pale-pink gums and an odorless breath are signs of good oral hygiene. Owners can use a toothbrush or a fingerbrush to clean the dog's teeth—but this task should only be done by adults.

# Family life

Welcome to the world! A mother's love sees her newborn puppies through their first weeks, with a lot of carrying and cleaning. She feeds the puppies milk for the first eight weeks of their lives.

**Mother dogs give birth to litters of three to nine puppies.**

**Nursing mother**
A pregnant dog eats her usual diet until the last two to three weeks of pregnancy. She tends to eat less as the puppies are about to be born. Once they are born, the mother increases her food intake so that she can produce milk to feed her babies.

The puppy can make noises and squeaks like a mouse.

The eyes are not fully open, so it cannot see very clearly.

## 1 week old

A newborn puppy is born deaf and blind. It spends a whopping 90 percent of the time asleep! When awake, it feeds on its mother's milk, which provides the pup with vital nutrients for its growth.

## 2–3 weeks old

The puppy's eyes open for the first time, and it can also hear now. It's able to stand and move a little, so this is when the fun starts! The puppy learns fast by copying its mom.

*The pup now begins to explore its surroundings.*

## 6 weeks old

The puppy stops feeding on its mother's milk and eats solid food. This is called weaning. The actual age when a pup is weaned can vary from breed to breed. Once weaned, the puppy eats three to four times a day.

## 3–4 weeks old

The pup develops a sense of smell. At three weeks, it eats its first solid food. It starts to play-fight with its siblings, and together they yelp and gently bite each other for fun.

*The young dog is now very energetic, and needs a lot of exercise and playtime.*

*The puppy learns from its mother that biting hard is not good.*

## 6–18 months old

The young dog may now refuse to be trained, or act as if it has forgotten previously learned commands. It becomes an adult between the ages of one to three years, depending on the size of the breed. The adult dog is less demanding, and tends to enjoy being trained.

# Puppy power

The early stages of life are an important time for learning, when puppies find out about the world. The way dogs behave as adults is affected by their life as puppies. It's important for owners to spend time with young dogs, so that they become confident adults.

Pups love to explore, so they need to be watched!

Puppies enjoy the company of their siblings or a human family. They love to play and make friends.

## Puppy training

Effective training helps puppies fit happily into their new homes. It's important for pups to learn not to jump on people, snatch food, or guard their belongings.

Puppies need to spend time with different people and animals. This is called socialization. Dogs that aren't socialized well as pups can have problems as adult dogs, such as feeling scared or biting.

As pups play together, they learn new rules and the best ways to behave. Training a puppy from a young age will encourage good behavior.

Puppies need routines with regular training, feeding, and playing to become confident and calm. As the pups get used to different objects, sounds, and scents, they become friendly and outgoing.

Unless playing or fighting, dogs hardly touch each other. It's important for owners to get young dogs used to being petted, but also to know when a dog wants to be left alone.

# Terriers

Terriers are named after the Latin word *terra*, which means "earth." These dogs were originally bred to chase vermin and badgers down holes. They have boundless energy, need a lot of exercise, and enjoy digging. It can be a challenge keeping up with a terrier!

The Black Russian Terrier has a dense, wavy coat.

## Black Russian Terrier

Bred by the Russian Army in the 1940s as a guard dog, the Black Russian Terrier is strong and brave. This terrier gets its large, muscular body from its parent breeds—Airedale Terriers, Rottweilers, and Giant Schnauzers.

### Fact file

- » **Origin:** Russia
- » **Height:** 26–30 in (66–77 cm)
- » **Color:** Black
- » **Character:** Friendly, brave, tough, and protective

Regular clipping helps to maintain the Irish Terrier's harsh, wiry coat.

### Fact file

- » **Origin:** Ireland
- » **Height:** 18–19 in (46–48 cm)
- » **Color:** Brown; red; brown and red
- » **Character:** Active and delightful

## Irish Terrier

This handsome breed can be easily identified by its bearded muzzle and bright-red coat. Always willing to please and a quick learner, the Irish Terrier makes a great family companion

## Boston Terrier

This dog is a mix of the Bulldog and a few other terrier breeds. This breed is from the city of Boston, Massachusetts. It is nicknamed the "American Gentleman" because its coat looks like a black-and-white tuxedo.

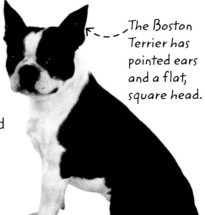

The Boston Terrier has pointed ears and a flat, square head.

### Fact file

» **Origin:** United States
» **Height:** 15–17 in (38–43 cm)
» **Color:** Black; brindle
» **Character:** Intelligent, alert, and docile

The Fox Terrier is white in color, but has tan or black markings on its face and body.

### Fact file

» **Origin:** United Kingdom
» **Height:** Up to 15 in (39 cm)
» **Color:** White with black or tan markings
» **Character:** Energetic, brave, and fun-loving

## Fox Terrier

The Fox Terrier was England's most popular breed in the 1800s. This breed is now loved for its cheerfulness. These dogs enjoy long walks and are always ready for a game of chase!

### Fact file

» **Origin:** Germany
» **Height:** 9–11 in (24–28 cm)
» **Color:** Black
» **Character:** Mischievous and lively

The Affenpinscher has a short muzzle and a long beard.

## Affenpinscher

The Affenpinscher, meaning "monkey-terrier," is named after its monkey-like face. Despite its size, this mini terrier is a brave guard dog. Affenpinschers learn quickly and love a lot of play.

# Airedale Terrier

Called "king of the terriers," this dog is one of the biggest in the group. The Airedale Terrier was first used to hunt badgers and otters. It now keeps busy by chasing and digging.

» **Origin:** United Kingdom
» **Height:** 22–24 in (56–61 cm)
» **Color:** Black and tan
» **Character:** Confident, clever, brave, and playful

Small, V-shaped ears fall forward just above the eyes.

An Airedale Terrier with British soldiers

## Service in war

Full of courage, the Airedale Terrier helped soldiers during World War I. These dogs were used to carry messages and necessary supplies to the troops. They also helped search for wounded soldiers.

This terrier has a dark-tan saddle.

The Airedale Terrier's wavy topcoat covers a fluffy undercoat.

Vermin, such as rats, were a big problem for English farmers in the 1800s. Airedale Terriers were bred to get rid of these pests.

Strong, long legs support the heavy body.

# Jack Russell Terrier

» **Origin:** United Kingdom
» **Height:** 13–14 in (33–36 cm)
» **Color:** White with a mix of black or brown
» **Character:** Happy, active, friendly, and independent

This terrier gets its name from the Reverend John Russell, who bred these dogs in the 1800s to hunt foxes. While the Jack Russell Terrier needs plenty of training and exercise, it is a wonderful family pet.

The tail is carried high unless the dog is resting.

Its ears are mostly dark, regardless of its coat color.

With a small body, this dog can easily move in an underground burrow.

Every Jack Russell has an individual pattern of markings.

## All in the family

The Parson Russell Terrier is the long-legged cousin of the Jack Russell. Like Jack Russells, they are high-energy and need firm handling. Both have a weatherproof coat.

*Parson Russell Terrier*

A Jack Russell named Bothie is the only dog to have traveled to both the North and South poles.

# West Highland White Terrier

**Fact file**

» **Origin:** Scotland
» **Height:** 10–11 in (25–28 cm)
» **Color:** White
» **Character:** Happy, active, friendly, and independent

Nicknamed the Westie, the West Highland White Terrier loves life and enjoys adventure. The breed was once used to hunt rats, and is now a lovable pet.

The Westie's powerful and strong body is packed with muscles.

It often tilts its head to one side, as if asking a question.

The terrier's fur has a rough top coat and a soft undercoat.

## Ancestral home

The Westie, originally named the Poltalloch Terrier, was first bred at Poltalloch House, the home of Colonel E.D. Malcolm in Scotland. Malcolm promoted the breed for many years, and it went on to become a popular pet.

Former house of the Malcolms

Westies love digging in the backyard and other open spaces, and can be very messy!

# Yorkshire Terrier

The Yorkshire Terrier was used to chase out rats and mice in the mills of England in the mid-1800s. Its long, shiny coat needs a lot of care, and the dog loves all the extra attention from its owner.

The Yorkshire Terrier has shiny eyes and an intelligent, alert expression on its face.

The dog has rich, bright, tan-colored hair.

## Mr. Famous

Movie star Audrey Hepburn's Yorkshire Terrier, Mr. Famous, was one of the first canine celebrities. He accompanied Hepburn to fashion events, and was even featured alongside her in the film *Funny Face*.

Audrey Hepburn and Mr. Famous

During World War II, a Yorkshire Terrier named Smoky pulled a telephone line through a 70-ft (21-m)-wide pipe in an airfield.

# Scottish Terrier

Lovingly called Scotties, Scottish Terriers are small, but powerful and agile. They make excellent watchdogs. In the past, these dogs were used to hunt rats, foxes, and badgers.

» **Origin:** United Kingdom
» **Height:** 10–11 in (25–28 cm)
» **Color:** Gold; black
» **Character:** Affectionate and watchful

Statue of Fala and his master

The earliest mention of this dog was by Scottish bishop John Lesley. He wrote about Scotties in his book *History of Scotland* from 1436 to 1561.

## Presidential pet

Former US President Franklin D. Roosevelt's Scottish Terrier, Fala, was his constant companion. Fala was such an important part of Roosevelt's life that he was honored with a statue in Washington, DC.

The dog has prominent, bushy eyebrows.

The Scottish Terrier has a long, dense beard.

The Scottie has a harsh, wiry coat that can be black or wheat-like in color.

# Border Terrier

The Border Terrier gets its name from where it was first bred—the area around the Scotland–England border. These hard-working dogs are small enough to chase foxes down narrow holes.

Its head resembles that of an otter.

The dog has a fairly short tail.

The Border Terrier has a short, strong muzzle.

It has tan hair on its legs that is a different color than the hair on its body.

**This terrier is loved for the mischievous expression on its face.**

A still from the film *Good Boy!*

## Canine actor

Being highly intelligent and easy to train, Border Terriers are a popular pick for films. They have starred in a number of blockbusters, including *Good Boy!*, *Cheaper by the Dozen*, and *Return to Oz*.

# Senses

Dogs have senses like humans, including sight, smell, hearing, taste, and touch. However, a dog's sense of smell is far more powerful than a human's—and there are other differences, too.

Dogs smell other animals to find out if they are friendly.

A dog can tilt, turn, raise, and lower its ears with the help of muscles inside them.

## Hearing

Dogs have a super sense of hearing. They can hear around four times better than a human can, and detect much quieter sounds than a human ear does.

A dog can see blue, yellow, and gray but not red or green.

## Sight

A dog's sight is not as developed as that of a human. Dogs tend to see better in dim light, such as at dawn or dusk, whereas humans see better in bright light.

## Touch

Adult dogs rarely touch or hold each other unless playing or fighting. They use their whiskers to sense things that they may not be able to see clearly.

*Puppies love to snuggle close to their mom and siblings.*

## Smell

A dog's sense of smell is like its own superpower. It is sixty times stronger than a human's, so a dog can smell a lot of things that a human can't.

*A dog's nose has 300 million smell receptors, but a human nose has only six million.*

*Dogs have special taste buds at the tip of their tongue to taste water.*

## Taste

While humans have over 9,000 taste buds, dogs only have around 1,700. This means that a dog's sense of taste is not as good as a human's.

## Ear emotions

A dog can express different feelings by the position of its ears. To understand a dog better, observe its overall body posture, including tail, eyes, and ears.

**Ears raised high: Strong interest**

**Ears pulled back: Willing to be friends**

**Ears flat down: Scared or worried**

A happy dog usually swings its tail more to the right than to the left.

A pup starts to "tail talk" with other dogs from as young as six weeks old.

# Tail talk

Dogs use their tails to express emotions. Whether short and stumpy or long and fluffy, watching the tail is the best way to know how a furry friend's day is going.

# Telltail signs

Dogs can express various emotions, such as excitement, nervousness, anger, and fear. Most of the time, they change the positions of their tails to show what they are feeling.

### Tucked tail
When the tail is tucked under the body, the dog is feeling scared or worried. It is best to give this pooch some space.

### Straight tail
A straight tail means the dog feels threatened. It is alert and defensive. Move back slowly, so that it knows you mean no harm.

### Upright tail
Something has caught this dog's eye. The tail stands upright to show excitement and interest. A chase could be on!

# Hounds

Many hounds were originally used as hunting dogs. There are two types of hound—sight hounds, which have superb vision, and scent hounds, which have an excellent sense of smell. Both will run after anything that catches their eye. Hang on tight when they're on a leash!

## Fact file

» **Origin:** France
» **Height:** 13–15 in (33–38 cm)
» **Color:** Variety of colors
» **Character:** Intelligent, calm, loyal, and affectionate

## Basset Hound

This short-legged breed makes a gentle family pet. The Basset Hound is a scent hound, known for its exceptional tracking skills. Once it picks up a scent, it may be hard to call it back!

The Basset Hound's ears sweep the scent toward its nose, to help it smell better.

## Fact file

» **Origin:** Switzerland
» **Height:** 18–22 in (45–57 cm)
» **Color:** Black and tan; two shades of brown
» **Character:** Sweet-tempered, lively, and determined

## Bruno Jura

The Bruno Jura originated in the Swiss Jura mountain region. This hunting dog is mostly used to catch hares in sloped terrains. With a good sense of smell, strong body, and ability to run fast, it loves to explore outdoors.

The Bruno Jura has rounded feet with tough pads.

# Finnish Hound

This large hound is very independent, which sometimes leads to stubbornness! The Finnish Hound has an athletic build, and loves to run around and chase balls.

The Finnish Hound has a large black area on its body, from neck to tail.

## Fact file
- » **Origin:** Finland
- » **Height:** 20–24 in (52–61 cm)
- » **Color:** Black, tan, and white
- » **Character:** Energetic, loving, and friendly

## Fact file
- » **Origin:** North Africa
- » **Height:** 24–28 in (61–72 cm)
- » **Color:** Fawn
- » **Character:** Elegant, active, and friendly

# Sloughi

The Sloughi is a sight hound, which was used in the past to guard flocks of sheep. It has a short, smooth coat, which allows its well-defined muscles to be seen. It also has striking, dark eyes.

The Sloughi has long, straight legs.

## Fact file
- » **Origin:** Malta
- » **Height:** 21–25 in (53–64 cm)
- » **Color:** Dark tan
- » **Character:** Affectionate and smart

# Pharaoh Hound

The Pharaoh Hound looks very similar to depictions of dogs in the tombs of ancient Egyptian kings and queens, or pharaohs. The breed is loved for its ability to learn to smile. Its ears and nose may even blush when it is happy or excited.

The Pharaoh Hound has a short, glossy coat.

# Norwegian Elkhound

The Norwegian Elkhound is the national dog of Norway, and looks like a small, cuddly wolf. It was once used to hunt large animals, such as moose and bears, but today it prefers to play in the snow.

» **Origin:** Norway
» **Height:** 19–20 in (49–52 cm)
» **Color:** Gray; silver
» **Character:** Strong, brave, protective, and bold

With its upright ears, the dog always looks alert.

The Norwegian Elkhound has a sturdy, strong body.

The dog has a black muzzle.

This breed's thick double coat keeps it warm in winter.

Nicknamed the "dog of the Vikings," the Elkhound was valued by the Viking people. It is often featured in Viking art, as well as in their legends.

## Weegie

Former US President Herbert Hoover's much-loved pet, Weegie, was a Norwegian Elkhound. The dog stayed in the White House throughout Hoover's tenure. After retiring, Hoover moved to Palo Alto in California, and Weegie accompanied him.

Hoover and his wife with Weegie

# Miniature Dachshund

The Miniature Dachshund was originally trained to crawl into tight burrows to sniff out rabbits and badgers. Even now, it loves following a scent, and may get too busy and ignore commands!

» **Origin:** Germany
» **Height:** 5–9 in (13–23 cm)
» **Color:** Any mix of brown, black, and cream
» **Character:** Brave, clever, independent, and lively

The word *Dachshund* means "badger dog" in German.

The Dachshund is known for its long, droopy ears.

This type of Dachshund has a smooth-haired coat.

The dog's stubby legs are good at digging.

This breed is nicknamed "wiener dog" after its long body and short legs.

## Coat types

Besides the smooth-haired type, these dogs can also be wire-haired or long-haired. The wire-haired types have a harsh, textured coat. The long-haired types have a long, flat coat with feathering.

Long-haired

Wire-haired

# Afghan Hound

The Afghan Hound's body is covered in soft fur to keep it warm in the freezing-cold mountains of Afghanistan. These dogs are calm indoors, but very active when it's time to play outside.

» **Origin:** Afghanistan
» **Height:** 25–29 in (64–74 cm)
» **Color:** Cream; brown; gray; black
» **Character:** Loyal, loving, protective, and sensitive

## Arriving in the US

Actor Herbert "Zeppo" Marx first spotted these hounds while shooting in England. Zeppo took two Afghan Hounds, named Asra of Ghazni and Westmill Omar, to the United States in 1931.

Herbert "Zeppo" Marx

When the Afghan Hound eats, owners often use ear stockings, called snoods, to cover its ears. This helps to keep the dog's extremely long ears clean.

The Afghan Hound's sharp eyesight helps it to hunt wild animals.

This breed has long, droopy ears.

The dog's flowing fur needs regular grooming to avoid knots and tangles.

# Greyhound

Sleek and powerful, Greyhounds are built for speed. They can run as fast as 45 mph (72 kph). Even so, they are sometimes called "the world's fastest couch potatoes" since they love sleeping and staying inside.

» **Origin:** United Kingdom
» **Height:** 27–30 in (69–76 cm)
» **Color:** Variety of colors
» **Character:** Lively and friendly

The Greyhound's neck is strong and muscular.

FASTEST DOG IN THE WORLD

The dog has a deep chest.

It has straight, long forelegs.

## Royal fans

King Henry VIII of England loved Greyhounds and had many of them in his royal court. His daughter, Queen Elizabeth I, loved them too.

King Henry VIII

In the past, Greyhounds were mostly used to hunt hares, but they could also chase down large animals, such as foxes and deer.

33

# Beagle

Hundreds of years ago, the Beagle was used to track rabbits. Also called "a nose on legs," this breed can still be spotted with its nose to the ground following interesting scents.

» **Origin:** United Kigdom
» **Height:** 13–16 in (33–40 cm)
» **Color:** Shades of brown, black, and white
» **Character:** Excitable, energetic, independent, and affectionate

Ears are long and droopy with rounded ends.

The Beagle's coat is soft and smooth.

Its body is compact, but powerful.

A newborn Beagle

## Changing colors

Beagles change color all their lives. Puppies usually start off as black and white. A few months later, the black patches turn brown. As they grow older, they continue to change color, but it's less obvious.

The famous comic character Snoopy™, from *Peanuts*, is a Beagle.

34

# Bloodhound

Bloodhounds are the best-known scent hounds in the world. They can even pick up smells that are several days old. This makes them well-suited to work as hunters, police dogs, and rescue dogs.

» **Origin:** Belgium
» **Height:** 23–27 in (58–69 cm)
» **Color:** Liver and tan; black and tan
» **Character:** Gentle and sociable

### Super cop
Bloodhounds have been used as police dogs since 1805. They can track down criminals and search for missing people. Evidence from bloodhound-tracking can be used in a US court of law.

A Bloodhound on the move

Its extremely long ears are set low on the head.

The Bloodhound has a waterproof coat, with smooth, short hair.

A powerful body allows the dog to work for long periods.

The Bloodhound was originally bred to hunt large animals, such as wild boar and deer.

The dog has a long, thick tail that narrows toward the end.

35

# Barks and yaps

From woofing, barking, and yelping, to howling, whining, and growling, dogs like to make themselves heard. Excited dogs will often keep repeating the same noise very quickly! Listen closely to these sounds to learn what they mean.

Dogs aren't the only animals that bark—foxes and sea lions do, too!

A few barks are welcoming, but a lot of barking can be a warning.

# Doggie talk

Dogs make a lot of sounds that can mean different things at different times. They use various noises when they are excited, scared, lonely, worried, or simply want some attention!

### Growl
Back off from a growling dog. This deep, throaty sound shows either unhappiness or irritation. A dog's growl is a warning to not come any closer.

### Yelp
The short, sharp sound, or yelp, usually means a dog has been surprised or hurt. It is best to stay calm and check to see what has startled it.

## Perfect pitch

A dog's barking pitch can range from low to high. Low-pitched noises can mean the dog is angry or scared. High-pitched sounds suggest excitement. Smaller dogs tend to make higher-pitched noises than bigger dogs.

### Yap
A repeated yapping sound comes from a needy dog wanting its owner's attention. If it's seeking attention without a reason, it is usually best to ignore the dog until it stops yapping.

# Sporting dogs

In the past, these dogs helped find and catch birds and other creatures. Today, they will fetch just about anything they come across. Like the hounds, many sporting dogs have an excellent sense of smell.

The Irish Setter has almond-shaped eyes and a kind look on its face.

### Fact file

» **Origin:** Ireland
» **Height:** 25–27 in (64–69 cm)
» **Color:** Red
» **Character:** Exuberant, active, and affectionate

## Irish Setter

Like other setters, the Irish Setter is named after its trait of "setting"—stopping and facing prey so that its owner can spot the animal. It continues to be a popular pet that loves to play and exercise.

The English Setter has a straight, furry tail that narrows toward the end.

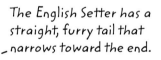

### Fact file

» **Origin:** United Kingdom
» **Height:** 24–27 in (61–69 cm)
» **Color:** Black and white; lemon and white; orange and white; brown and white; tricolor
» **Character:** Reliable and quiet

## English Setter

Easy to train and gentle with children, the English Setter is a lovable family pet. This breed is the oldest of all setters, dating back at least four hundred years.

The Labrador Retriever has a waterproof coat.

## Fact file

» **Origin:** Canada
» **Height:** 22 in (55–57 cm)
» **Color:** Black; yellow; chocolate
» **Character:** Responsive and friendly

# Labrador Retriever

The ancestors of the Labrador Retriever were used by Canadian fishermen to pull in fishing nets. Today, this dog is best known as a great family dog that loves to please its owner. It enjoys long walks and is fond of water.

## Fact file

» **Origin:** United States
» **Height:** 15–18 in (38–45 cm)
» **Color:** Brown
» **Character:** Active, loving, loyal, and energetic

# American Water Spaniel

The American Water Spaniel is the state dog of Wisconsin. Its handsome, curly coat is very unusual. This high-energy explorer loves splashing in water, which is why it is also known as a water dog.

The American Water Spaniel's webbed feet are perfect for swimming.

# German Spaniel

In earlier days, this breed helped bring back quail. German Spaniels enjoy the water, and are happiest when given a task. They love spending time with their owners.

The German Spaniel has a long, thick, and wavy coat.

## Fact file

» **Origin:** Germany
» **Height:** 17–21 in (44–54 cm)
» **Color:** White; fawn; brown; liver; gray; red
» **Character:** Gentle and obedient

# Weimaraner

This dog is nicknamed the "gray ghost" after its unusual shiny, gray coat and eyes. The Weimaraner can have a short- or long-haired coat. In the past, it was used to track deer and wolves.

» **Origin:** Germany
» **Height:** 22–27 in (56–69 cm)
» **Color:** Silver-gray
» **Character:** Clever, fearless, loving, and loyal

A Weimaraner on the go

## Fast runners

The Weimaraner has firm, compact feet that enable it to run at fast speeds. This dog has a lot of energy and needs plenty of exercise. It is best-suited to open spaces where it can run freely.

This breed's light-colored eyes can darken when it is excited.

The Weimaraner has a strong, muscular body.

This clever dog is also called "the dog with a human brain."

# Golden Retriever

This breed was named after its ability to retrieve, or fetch, ducks from ponds, which was what it was once used for. The Golden Retriever is a strong swimmer and enjoys water.

The Golden Retriever has soft, floppy ears.

Its fur can be flat or wavy.

**Goldendoodle**

The Goldendoodle is a mix of the Golden Retriever and Standard Poodle. It is a very popular pet.

This dog has a fluffy tail.

The feet are round and short.

## Guide dogs

Golden Retrievers are sweet-tempered and easy to train. They make one of the most popular guide dogs, which help people with visual impairments.

A Retriever guiding a visually impaired man

41

# American Cocker Spaniel

The long, silky coat and big, dark eyes of the American Cocker Spaniel make it a very popular pet. These dogs are quick and energetic, and need a lot of exercise.

» **Origin:** United States
» **Height:** 13–15 in (34–39 cm)
» **Color:** Variety of colors
» **Character:** Affectionate and playful

The American Cocker Spaniel was especially good at hunting woodcocks. This is how the dog got its name.

The top of its head is round, with prominent eyebrows.

The neck is long enough to help the dog's nose sniff the ground.

Its long hair needs daily grooming to avoid tangles.

English Cocker Spaniel

## Similar yet different

At first, it may be difficult to tell the difference between the English and the American Cocker Spaniel. The English variety is taller and has a less dense coat than its American cousin.

# English Springer Spaniel

The English Springer Spaniel gets its name from the way it springs, or surprises, birds into flight. This breed gets along well with children, other dogs, and even cats.

Fact file

» **Origin:** United Kingdom
» **Height:** 18–22 in (46–56 cm)
» **Color:** Black and white; liver and white
» **Character:** Bright, sensitive, and sociable

The English Springer Spaniel's coat is thick, straight, and weatherproof.

Its furry tail is carried below the level of the back.

This dog's feet are well-rounded and compact.

## Painted pals

Many artworks from the sixteenth and seventeenth centuries feature dogs that resemble the English Springer Spaniel. Back then, dogs were used in art as a symbol of loyalty.

A seventeenth-century Dutch painting

This breed is used by the police as a sniffer dog. It uses scent to sniff out banned items, such as explosives.

# Chesapeake Bay Retriever

Also known as the Chessie, this breed was used to fetch waterfowl in the rough waters of the Chesapeake Bay. The Chesapeake Bay Retriever has webbed feet that make it an excellent swimmer.

» **Origin:** United States
» **Height:** 21—26 in (53—66 cm)
» **Color:** Gold; red; brown
» **Character:** Calm, gentle, and intelligent

The Chesapeake Bay Retriever has a medium-length, curved tail.

STATE DOG OF MARYLAND

The double coat is waterproof.

## True Grit

A Chesapeake Bay Retriever named True Grit is the mascot of the University of Maryland, Baltimore County. Students rub the nose of a statue of the dog for good luck before exams.

*Statue of True Grit*

44

# Brittany

In the past, the Brittany helped people to hunt. It could pick up the scent of animals and lead people after them. The dog was also skilled at bringing back the game. Today, it makes a gentle family pet.

» **Origin:** France
» **Height:** 19–20 in (47–51 cm)
» **Color:** Orange and white; liver and white; black and white; black, tan, and white
» **Character:** Loyal, active, and friendly

The Brittany has oval, dark eyes.

Its orange-and-white coat is dense and slightly wavy.

The front legs of this dog are very furry.

A Brittany puppy

## Born tailless

Brittany puppies are one of the very few breeds that are sometimes born without tails. Other Brittany puppies are born with a stubby tail that is up to 4 in (10 cm) long.

Brittany

This breed gets its name from the French region of Brittany. The first Brittany was born here hundreds of years ago.

45

# Italian Spinone

The Italian Spinone has taken part in the human sport of hunting for centuries. It can follow ground scents, as well as those in the air. Its wire-haired coat offers protection in thorny shrubs and icy water.

**Fact file**

» **Origin:** Italy
» **Height:** 24–26 in (61–66 cm)
» **Color:** White; white and orange; white and brown
» **Character:** Responsive, loyal, and relaxed

—The Italian Spinone has a sturdy back.

A thick coat lies close to the body, with a dense undercoat.

In the 1470s, Italian artist Andrea Mantegna painted a dog similar to the Spinone in his mural *The Court of Gonzaga.*

Its ears are triangular and droopy.

## Multitasker

The Italian Spinone is known to be one of the best hunting dogs. This dog can both point its muzzle toward the prey to indicate its position and jump into water to retrieve it.

Italian Spinone jumping into water

This dog gets its name from *prunus spinosa,* a thorny plant that grows in Italy.

# Blue Picardy Spaniel

The Blue Picardy Spaniel was mostly used in marshlands to bring back wading birds called snipes from the water. These dogs have a calm nature and love spending time with children.

The Blue Picardy Spaniel has a lighter-colored patch on its head.

The long, droopy ears are covered with wavy hair.

Originally a water dog, the Blue Picardy Spaniel loves to swim and splash around.

## Striking coat

This dog has an attractive coat, which is blue-gray with black patches all over. The pups, however, tend to be white-gray at birth. The color fills in as they grow.

Close-up of the coat

The dog has webbed toes that help it to swim.

# Working dogs

These breeds are trained to carry out different tasks for people. They might keep watch, pull heavy loads, or herd animals. Some of them even have jobs, such as helping with emergency rescues.

The Czechoslovakian Wolfdog has pointed, triangular ears.

## Fact file

» **Origin:** Czech Republic
» **Height:** 24–26 in (60–65 cm)
» **Color:** Gray
» **Character:** Docile and fearless

## Czechoslovakian Wolfdog

This Wolfdog is a cross between the German Shepherd and gray wolf. The breed looks a lot like wolves—in their body shape, coat, and facial markings. Although uncertain around strangers, Czechoslovakian Wolfdogs enjoy the company of their owners.

## Dutch Shepherd

This dog is mostly found in the Netherlands. It is used as a police and guide dog. The Dutch Shepherd is also very affectionate, and makes a wonderful pet.

The Dutch Shepherd's thick coat can be rough or smooth, with varied markings.

## Fact file

» **Origin:** The Netherlands
» **Height:** 22–24 in (43–46 cm)
» **Color:** Sandy gold; red chestnut
» **Character:** Alert, obedient, and loyal

The Neapolitan Mastiff has a short, dense, and shiny coat.

This breed played Fang, Hagrid the half-giant's pet, in the Harry Potter™ films.

## Fact file

» **Origin:** Italy
» **Height:** 24–30 in (60–75 cm)
» **Color:** Variety of colors
» **Character:** Protective and alert

# Neapolitan Mastiff

Because of its strong build, the Neapolitan Mastiff was used to guard and pull heavy loads. Today, these dogs are admired for their power, as well as their willingness to please their owners.

## Fact file

» **Origin:** France
» **Height:** 26–28 in (65–70 cm)
» **Color:** White; white with tan patches
» **Character:** Protective, calm, and loyal

# Pyrenean Mountain Dog

In the past, this dog was used to guard livestock and pull sleds. Despite its large size and strength, it does not need much exercise. A loving companion for children, this breed is popular with families.

The Pyrenean Mountain Dog has a thick, wavy, and long coat.

# Saint Bernard

These gentle giants have been used as rescue dogs for hundreds of years. Saint Bernards make wonderful pets, too, but they need a home with large spaces to allow for their size.

### Fact file

» **Origin:** Switzerland
» **Height:** 28–30 in (70–75 cm)
» **Color:** Brown and white
» **Character:** Lively, friendly, loving, and loyal

The Saint Bernard's skull is massive and slightly curved.

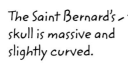

Saint Bernards are calm and alert. This makes them good "nanny dogs" for children.

## Rescue dogs in the Swiss Alps

For many centuries, monks at a hospice in the Swiss Alps of Switzerland kept Saint Bernards. These powerful dogs sniffed out people stuck in snowstorms.

The Saint Bernards of the hospice

The thick coat can be rough or smooth, with varied markings.

# Siberian Husky

The Siberian Husky was first used to pull sleds for local people in snowy Siberia. It is strong, determined, and can run long distances. It is now a popular pet.

» **Origin:** Siberia
» **Height:** 20–24 in (51–60 cm)
» **Color:** Varieties of black, gray, silver, and white
» **Character:** Clever, friendly, reliable, and playful

Huskies have blue or brown eyes that are often alert.

This breed has an athletic body shape and powerful legs.

During WWII, planes sometimes crashed in the frozen lands of the Arctic Circle. The US Army sent out Huskies to bring back injured pilots.

Leonhard Seppala standing on sea ice holding his dogs.

## Alaskan heroes

In 1925, Siberian Husky sled dogs helped bring lifesaving medicine to Nome, Alaska. The region was affected by a serious disease, and the only available medicine was nearly 600 miles (1,000 km) away. A sled-team driver named Leonhard Seppala led a team of twenty Huskies on the mission.

The tough, furry feet are ideal for covering hard ground.

# Komondor

The Komondor looks like a large mop on legs. Its coat consists of long cords that cover it from head to tail. This dog was originally used to protect sheep, goats, and cattle from wolves and bears.

» **Origin:** Hungary
» **Height:** 24–31 in (60–80 cm)
» **Color:** White
» **Character:** Protective and loyal

Its dark eyes are partially covered by the coat.

Daily grooming is needed to maintain its corded coat.

The Komondor has large, powerful feet.

## Canine twin

The Puli is a sheepdog that resembles the Komondor, but is much smaller. Komondors protect the sheep, whereas Pulis only help to herd them.

A Puli

Komondors were good at protecting sheep because they could hide among the herd and surprise attacking predators.

# Bernese Mountain Dog

Bernese Mountain Dogs can do various jobs, such as herding livestock, pulling carts, and guarding animals. Recently, they have also proved to be great therapy dogs.

» **Origin:** Switzerland
» **Height:** 23–28 in (58–70 cm)
» **Color:** Black; brown; white
» **Character:** Loyal, clever, affectionate, and gentle

Bernese Mountain Dog pulling a milk cart

The Bernese Mountain Dog has a broad head with a white patch on it.

## Cart dogs

Bernese Mountain Dogs were once used to pull carts of milk and cheese from the mountains down to the valleys. This earned them the nickname "cheese dog."

It can pull up to 1,000 lb (455 kg)— ten times its own weight.

Thick, long fur provides a layer of warmth in the mountains.

In German, this dog is called *berner sennenhund*, which means "Bernese alpine herdsman's dog."

53

# Briard

The Briard is a popular dog in France, where people once used it to herd and protect farm animals. This large dog is extremely protective of its owners and makes a good watchdog.

» **Origin:** France
» **Height:** 23–27 in (58–69 cm)
» **Color:** Gray; fawn; black
» **Character:** Confident, smart, and loyal

At a glance, it might look as if the Briard has its hair in pigtails. This is because its ears are covered with hair, and set high on a rectangular head.

The Briard has a square-shaped muzzle and a black nose.

This breed has a long, wavy coat.

The dog has strong, slightly rounded feet.

## Winning over

Former US President Thomas Jefferson was not always fond of dogs. This changed when French aristocrat and military officer Lafayette sent Briards to guard Jefferson's livestock.

Thomas Jefferson

# Boxer

This family dog is courageous and doesn't give up easily. It's also a popular choice for police work, military missions, and guard work. Boxers are so playful that they make great companions for children, too.

The Boxer has an expressive face with dark-brown eyes and a wrinkled forehead.

There are white markings on the chest, face, and legs.

While playing, Boxers often stand on their back legs and punch out with their front paws. This action resembles that of a human boxer, and got the dog its name.

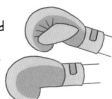

A Boxer with its tongue out

## Long tongues

Boxers are known to have the longest tongues of all dog breeds. A Boxer named Brandy once held the record for "Longest Tongue on a Dog." Her tongue was 17 in (43 cm) in length—almost four times longer than a human tongue.

# Newfoundland

In the past, the Newfoundland would jump into the water to bring back nets for fishermen. This large dog is calm around kids, and is best-suited for bigger homes.

» **Origin:** Canada
» **Height:** 26–28 in (66–71 cm)
» **Color:** Black; dark brown
» **Character:** Gentle and friendly

The Newfoundland has a massive head.

## Water warrior

Because of its exceptional swimming skills, this breed is used for water rescue missions. The dog's webbed feet and waterproof coat enable it to swim far distances.

A Newfoundland on a rescue mission

In the 1800s, a Newfoundland named Seaman joined the explorers Meriwether Lewis and William Clark on a daring expedition across America.

It has a flat, rough, and slightly oily coat.

# Great Dane

Nicknamed the "Apollo of dogs" after the Greek god, this dog is admired for its strength and grace. Originally bred to hunt boars, the Great Dane now makes a wonderful family pet.

**Fact file**

» **Origin:** Germany
» **Height:** 28–30 in (71–76 cm)
» **Color:** Black and white; blue; black; brindle; fawn
» **Character:** Affectionate, patient, and dependable

The Great Dane has triangular, droopy ears.

A Great Dane with its owner

The popular cartoon dog Scooby-Doo™ was inspired by the Great Dane.

This breed can be as tall as 7 ft (2 m) when standing on its back legs.

## Standing tall

The Great Dane is the world's tallest dog. This dog can tower over most people when it stands on its hind legs. Despite its gigantic size, the Great Dane is gentle and loves human company.

# Dogs with jobs

Many types of dog can be trained to help care for their owners. These service dogs assist people who may have a disability or illness. Here are some of the many different jobs that dogs do.

## Guide dogs

These dogs help people who are visually impaired. Whether in the home or on a busy street, they lead their owners around with care.

## Allergy-detection dogs

Many people have serious allergies to different foods. Allergy-detection dogs are trained to sniff out specific smells, such as peanuts, before alerting their owners to the danger.

## Medical-alert-and-detection dogs

Medical-alert-and-detection dogs know the signs when people with serious illnesses are about to collapse. These dogs make their owners seek help. Some dogs can also sniff medical samples to detect diseases like cancer.

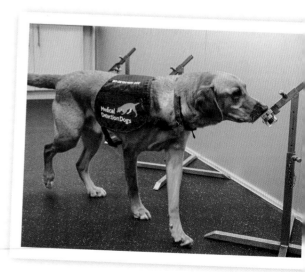

# Mobility-assistance dogs

f someone uses a wheelchair or has to stay in bed, mobility-assistance dogs can help out. These dogs do many jobs, such as opening doors and helping their owners shop.

# Hero dogs

The most talented and brave canines are true heroes. Dogs often work in dangerous situations to save lives, whether performing rescues in emergencies or discovering harmful items.

### Detection dogs
Doggy detectives are trained to hunt for things. Airports and border controls rely on them to find to find explosives and other banned items.

### Rescue dogs
Search-and-rescue dogs help find people in the snow after a snowstorm, or in the rubble of a collapsed building.

# Hearing dogs

Trained dogs let people with a hearing impairment know when there is a sound, such as a doorbell. They also pick up on danger signs, such as smoke alarms, and alert their owners.

### Soldiers' companions
Many armies and navies use trained guard dogs to protect their soldiers. These dogs can sniff out dangerous bombs and mines.

# Herding dogs

Herding dogs are a type of working dog that were first used on farms to round up sheep and cattle. As pets, they still like to take charge and will try to herd their owners.

The Icelandic Sheepdog has a short, compact muzzle.

### Fact file

- » **Origin:** Iceland
- » **Height:** 17–18 in (42–46 cm)
- » **Color:** Gray; black; dark brown or chocolate; tan with white markings
- » **Character:** Smart, cheerful, and vocal

## Icelandic Sheepdog

This tough, little dog is related to the Husky. The Icelandic Sheepdog is a fast, muscular breed with a loud bark—perfect for herding livestock.

### Fact file

- » **Origin:** Switzerland
- » **Height:** 17–20 in (42–50 cm)
- » **Color:** Black; black, white, and tan; black, white, and yellow
- » **Character:** Confident and energetic

The Entlebucher Mountain Dog has reddish-brown markings above its eyes.

## Entlebucher Mountain Dog

The Entlebucher Mountain Dog is a huge Swiss breed first used to herd cattle. Wary of strangers, this lively dog can be quite protective of its family members.

## Fact file

- » **Origin:** Belgium
- » **Height:** 22–26 in (56–66 cm)
- » **Color:** Black
- » **Character:** Obedient and loyal

# Groenendael

The Groenendael is a handsome breed with a striking black coat. A curious dog, it loves exploring outside. This dog needs firm but kind training.

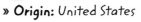

The Groenendael has a long, rough, and straight outer coat.

The Australian Shepherd's white hair extends across its neck, chest, and legs.

## Fact file

- » **Origin:** United States
- » **Height:** 18–23 in (46–58 cm)
- » **Color:** Black; blue and gray; red; red and cream
- » **Character:** Obedient, affectionate, and playful

## Australian Shepherd

This ranch dog was first bred in the US. The name comes from its ancestors, which were used by shepherds who moved to Australia in the late nineteenth century, and then later back to the US.

The Belgian Tervuren has shorter hair on its face than on its body.

## Fact file

- » **Origin:** Belgium
- » **Height:** 22–26 in (56–66 cm)
- » **Color:** Fawn and black; gray and black
- » **Character:** Intelligent and energetic

## Belgian Tervuren

Named after the village where it was bred, the Belgian Tervuren has strong protective instincts. Since it is easy to train, this dog makes a great police or sniffer dog. However, it has a long coat that needs a lot of grooming.

61

# Pembroke Welsh Corgi

**Fact file**

» **Origin:** United Kingdom
» **Height:** 10–12 in (25–30 cm)
» **Color:** Red; black; brown
» **Character:** Loyal, clever, friendly, and fun-loving

In the past, the Pembroke Welsh Corgi was used as a guard dog and cattle herder in Wales. This small dog is quick and strong. It enjoys spending time with its owner.

According to Welsh legend, fairies used to ride into battle on Corgis. The furry patch over their shoulders is called the fairy saddle.

The Pembroke Welsh Corgi has a fox-like face with huge ears.

It is usually light brown with a white chest.

The Corgi has short legs.

Queen Elizabeth II with her Corgis

## The Queen's favorites

Queen Elizabeth II has owned around thirty Corgis during her reign. These royal dogs have special baskets in their own room in Buckingham Palace. They eat meals prepared by a chef.

# Old English Sheepdog

The shaggy Old English Sheepdog needs a regular haircut to avoid fur covering its eyes. It was originally used to guide cattle to farmers' markets. This dog is loved for its sweet nature and good behavior.

» **Origin:** United Kingdom
» **Height:** 22–24 in (56–61 cm)
» **Color:** Gray and white
» **Character:** Clever, loving, playful, and friendly

This dog's eyes are hidden by its coat.

Its long, thick coat must be brushed with care.

This dog has a loud and unique bark that sounds like two pots banging against each other.

Thomas the Dulux dog

## Dulux dog
Old English Sheepdogs have been featured in advertisements for the international paint brand Dulux™ for over sixty years. Some even have their own chauffeurs!

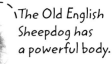

The Old English Sheepdog has a powerful body.

63

# Border Collie

This dog works like a shepherd guiding its flock. When herding sheep, the Border Collie can run more than 50 miles (80 km) a day. At sheepdog competitions, Border Collies and other breeds compete to see who can herd sheep the best.

**Fact file**

» **Origin:** United Kingdom
» **Height:** 20–21 in (50–53 cm)
» **Color:** Black and white
» **Character:** Alert, loyal, energetic, and reliable

Border Collie rounding up a goose

## Herding geese

Border Collies are often trained to gather geese into a small area on farms. These dogs fix their eyes on the geese in a strong stare and walk toward them. This is enough warning for the birds. The Collies are taught not to harm the geese.

—The Border Collie's ears are set apart.

The fastest 330 ft (100 m) on a skateboard by a dog is 19.65 seconds. This record was achieved by a Border Collie mix, Jumpy, in 2013.

This breed's athletic body is built for speed.

This dog's fluffy tail is set low on its body.

Its patterned fur can be rough or smooth.

# German Shepherd

> **Origin:** Germany
> **Height:** 23–25 in (58–63 cm)
> **Color:** Variety of colors
> **Character:** Intelligent and loyal

The German Shepherd is known for its guarding and tracking skills. It is used for many jobs, including police and military work, search-and-rescue missions, and guiding visually impaired people.

This breed has large, firm, and erect ears.

The head narrows towards the nose.

Rin Tin Tin on a film set

This breed was used as one of the first guide dogs in the US.

### Rin Tin Tin

A German Shepherd named Rin Tin Tin was rescued during World War I by a US soldier. The dog went on to become a famous canine actor, being featured in twenty-eight Hollywood films during his lifetime.

The German Shepherd has a thick coat.

# Nonsporting dogs

These varied dogs are those that don't fit into any of the other groups. This means they have a huge range of looks, from fluffy to wrinkly. With so many different breeds, there is something for everyone.

 **Fact file**

- » **Origin:** The Netherlands
- » **Height:** 17–18 in (43–46 cm)
- » **Color:** Black with cream markings
- » **Character:** Affectionate, lively, and outgoing

## Keeshond

In the eighteenth century, the Keeshond was used as a watchdog by river boatmen and farmers in Holland. This breed mixes well with people and other pets.

The Keeshond has short, cream-colored hair on its lower legs and feet.

The Norwegian Lundehund's dense coat sheds heavily.

## Chinese Shar-Pei

This dog dislikes the cold and prefers to stay inside. The Chinese Shar-Pei gets upset by strangers, so a family setting suits it best. It gives its owner a lot of love and loyalty.

### Fact file

- » **Origin:** China
- » **Height:** 18–20 in (46–51 cm)
- » **Color:** Variety of colors
- » **Character:** Affectionate, loyal, confident, and clever

_The Chinese Shar-Pei is known for its wrinkly skin._

The Chinese call the Shar-Pei's snub nose a "butterfly-cookie nose."

### Fact file

- » **Origin:** France
- » **Height:** 10–13 in (25–33 cm)
- » **Color:** Variety of colors
- » **Character:** Loving, energetic, friendly, and intelligent

_The Löwchen's coat is often long at the front and clipped at the back._

### Fact file

- » **Origin:** Norway
- » **Height:** 13–15 in (32–38 cm)
- » **Color:** White; gray; black; red
- » **Character:** Protective, responsive, and independent

## Norwegian Lundehund

In the past, this dog would climb steep cliffs to hunt for puffins. Unlike other dogs, the Norwegian Lundehund is extremely flexible. It can run quickly and easily.

## Löwchen

This dog was named after the mane-like hair on its head and neck—in German, _löwchen_ means "little lion." Its compact size and nonshedding coat make the Löwchen an easy-to-manage family pet.

# Dalmatian

Famous for its spotted coat and fun-loving personality, the Dalmatian is a much-loved family pet. This dog even has spots inside its mouth. It is a high-energy breed and needs a lot of exercise.

» **Origin:** Unknown
» **Height:** 22–24 in (56–61 cm)
» **Color:** White with black or brown spots
» **Character:** Friendly, active, energetic, and loyal

Dalmatian with a firefighter

## Fire-station dogs

In the past, the Dalmatian ran alongside carriages, guarding the passengers. Later, these dogs became fire-station dogs in the United States. They ran ahead of horse-drawn fire engines to clear the way.

Dalmatian puppies are white when they are born. The spots appear after around six weeks.

Every Dalmatian has a unique pattern of spots.

Most Dalmatians have black spots, but they can also be brown.

The feet are round and cat-like.

# Poodle

Originally, the Poodle was used to retrieve birds from rivers and lakes. This breed still enjoys being in water. In France, it is called the *Caniche*, which means "duck dog." The Poodle has a non-shedding coat.

## Fact file

» **Origin:** Germany, France
» **Height:** Toy: Up to 11 in (28 cm); Miniature: 11–15 in (28–38 cm); Medium: 15–18 in (38–45 cm)
» **Color:** Varied, but mostly black, white, cream, and gray
» **Character:** Alert, clever, and loving

Its fluffy ears are set low on the face.

The Poodle's tail is carried away from its body.

**The Poodle is the national dog breed of France.**

This breed has a sharp sense of smell and is used to hunt truffles. Truffles are a type of fungus, and are one of the most expensive foods.

The fur on a Poodle's tail and feet is often clipped short.

## Hound hairstyles

Poodles can be seen with a variety of striking hairstyles. In the past, these dogs were given a traditional Poodle cut—puffs of hair were kept around the joints and upper body to keep them warm.

# Chow Chow

In the past, the Chow Chow was used for guarding cattle, and pulling carts and sleds. This dog is known for its dense coat, lion-like mane, and blue-black tongue.

» **Origin:** China
» **Height:** 18–22 in (46–56 cm)
» **Color:** Cream; gold; red; blue; black
» **Character:** Independent, alert, and loyal

Sigmund Freud with Jo-Fi

## Dog doctor

Famous doctor Sigmund Freud had a Chow Chow named Jo-Fi, who assisted him during appointments. Jo-Fi's presence helped patients stay calm, especially children.

This dog's tiny ears are mostly covered with fur.

The Chow Chow's fluffy tail curves over its back.

The Chow Chow has a cat-like personality. This breed is more independent than most dogs.

The fur on the chest and back of the legs can be lighter.

# Shiba Inu

This is the most popular companion dog in Japan. Pointed ears and a red coat make the Shiba Inu look like a fox. This dog is known to scream when it is scared, nervous, or unhappy.

- » **Origin:** Japan
- » **Height:** 15–16 in (37–40 cm)
- » **Color:** Black and tan; white; red
- » **Character:** Alert, active, and cheerful

The Shiba Inu's small, triangular ears tilt forward.

This dog's bushy tail is curled and carried high.

**In Japanese, the word *Inu* means "dog."**

## Brushwood dog

In Japanese, *Shiba* means "brushwood," or "fallen branches." This name may describe the bushy terrain in which the dog once hunted, or the red color of the dog's coat—which is similar to some types of tree branches.

Close-up of red brushwood

The coat is easy to maintain since it does not get tangled.

71

# Toy dogs

Some toy dog breeds don't grow very big, while others are miniature versions of larger dogs. These dogs are intelligent and full of energy. Suited to living in apartments, they are popular home pets and often enjoy sitting in their owner's lap.

## Fact file

» **Origin:** China
» **Height:** Up to 11 in (27 cm)
» **Color:** Variety of colors
» **Character:** Intelligent and outgoing

The Shih Tzu has a long moustache.

## Shih Tzu

The Shih Tzu is one of the most loved toy dogs in the world. Although this dog sheds very little, its long coat needs to be groomed every day. In the past, this breed was a favorite with Chinese royalty.

The Japanese Chin has long hair on its ears.

## Fact file

» **Origin:** Japan
» **Height:** 8–11 in (20–28 cm)
» **Color:** Black and white; red and white
» **Character:** Extrovert and lively

## Japanese Chin

This toy dog was used especially as a lap warmer for the women of Japan's Imperial Palace. Ancestors of this dog may have been a royal gift from China to the Emperor of Japan. The Japanese Chin is comfortable in small living spaces.

# Papillon

The Papillon is named after the French word for "butterfly," because of the shape of its ears. This breed was once popular with European royalty, and can be seen in many paintings of queens and princesses.

## Fact file

» **Origin:** France
» **Height:** 8–11 in (20–28 cm)
» **Color:** Variety of colors
» **Character:** Lively and clever

↑ The Papillon has a silky topcoat.

The Pomeranian has a fox-like face.

## Fact file

» **Origin:** Germany
» **Height:** 9–11 in (22–28 cm)
» **Color:** Any solid color (no black or white shading)
» **Character:** Cheerful and smart

# Pomeranian

The Pomeranian gets its name from the historical region of Pomerania (in modern-day Poland and Germany), where it was first bred to herd sheep. This small dog has a lot of confidence.

The Chihuahua has large, bat-like ears.

## Fact file

» **Origin:** Mexico
» **Height:** 6–9 in (15–23 cm)
» **Color:** Variety of colors
» **Character:** Charming, bold, and graceful

# Chihuahua

There are two varieties of the Chihuahua—long-haired and short-haired. This tiny dog has a strong personality and is a devoted companion. It enjoys short walks and playing games.

# Chinese Crested Dog

The Chinese Crested Dog has fur only on its head, feet, and tail. This energetic breed loves climbing, jumping, and digging. However, its skin is delicate, and needs protection from extreme heat and cold.

## The hairy one

The powderpuff variety of this breed has a long, soft coat. These dogs need regular grooming to prevent tangles. A single litter can have both coat varieties.

**Long coat type**

The Chinese Crested Dog has large, erect ears.

Its smooth skin needs to be cleaned with a gentle shampoo.

This dog has a sock of white hair on the lower legs and feet.

In the past, the Chinese Crested Dog was used for hunting rats on Chinese ships.

# French Bulldog

Small but sturdy, the French Bulldog has large, bat-like ears. This breed requires a lot of exercise, and gets along well with people and other animals.

The ears are wider at the base, and rounded at the tip.

When a baby orangutan was abandoned in a zoo in England, a French Bulldog took care of it. They became great friends.

The French Bulldog has a strong neck.

A group of women lace makers

## Lap warmers

In the mid-1800s, dogs similar to this breed were used as lap warmers by lace makers in England. The workers took their pets to France when they moved there for work. These dogs became the ancestors of the first French Bulldogs.

The French Bulldog is also called a Frenchie.

This dog has a very short and soft coat.

75

# Pekingese

The Pekingese has been around for hundreds of years. It was a favorite breed of the Chinese royal family, who sometimes kept the dog in the sleeves of their flowing robes. In fact, for a long time it was forbidden for anyone else to own one.

» **Origin:** China
» **Height:** 6–9 in (15–23 cm
» **Color:** Varieties of black, brown, gray, and cream
» **Character:** Clever, loving, stubborn, and proud

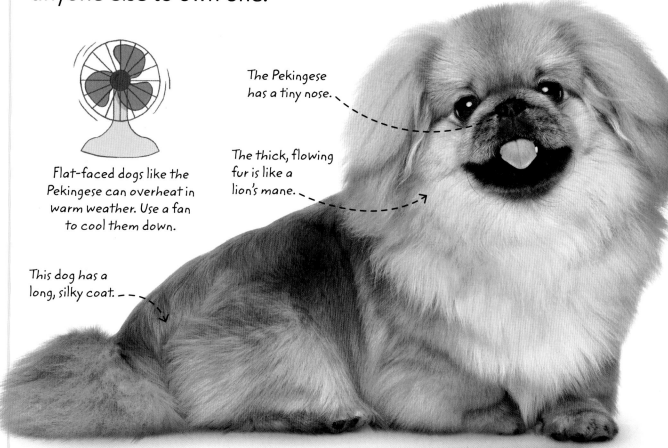

Flat-faced dogs like the Pekingese can overheat in warm weather. Use a fan to cool them down.

The Pekingese has a tiny nose.

The thick, flowing fur is like a lion's mane.

This dog has a long, silky coat.

## Lion dog

According to a Chinese legend, a lion and marmoset once fell in love. The lion asked the gods to shrink his body so he would be the same size as the tiny marmoset. Together they created the first Pekingese, also known as a "lion dog."

Historical painting showing Pekingese dogs

76

# Pug

The Pug is a cheerful family pet. It enjoys the company of children and other animals. This breed was originally used as a lapdog by Chinese emperors and nobles.

> **Origin:** China
> **Height:** 10–11 in (25–28 cm)
> **Color:** Silver; black; apricot
> **Character:** Playful, intelligent, and willful

In Holland, the pug is called a *mopshond.*

The Pug has a broad chest.

This breed's tail is curled tightly.

## Changing faces

The Pug's features have undergone big changes since the nineteenth century. Earlier, the Pug had a longer muzzle and legs. Its body was more athletic. Over time, the dog was bred to have a flat face and nose.

A Pug in 1890

77

# Bichon Frise

This breed is known for its soft, curly coat. Around the thirteenth century, the Bichon Frise was popular in the French, Spanish, and Italian royal courts. This fun-loving dog is a delight to be around.

» **Origin:** Tenerife
» **Height:** 9–12 in (23–31 cm
» **Color:** White
» **Character:** Active and friendly

Bolognese Bichon

## Close cousin

The Bolognese also belongs to the Bichon family, but it is smaller and less popular. The Bolognese is also shier than its Bichon cousin.

The Bichon Tenerife was first bred on the island of Tenerife. It is the main ancestor of the Bichon Frise.

Canary Islands

The Bichon Frise's tail curls over its back.

The fluffy ears are almost hidden by the long coat.

This dog has round feet.

78

# Cavalier King Charles Spaniel

This dog was named after King Charles II of England and his pet Spaniels. Known as the "king of the toy dogs," the Cavalier King Charles Spaniel loves action and affection at all times.

**Fact file**

» **Origin:** United Kingdom
» **Height:** 12–13 in (30–33 cm)
» **Color:** Brown and white; black; brown
» **Character:** Loving, playful, clever, and sociable

The Cavalier King Charles Spaniel has big, brown eyes.

Long ears hang down either side of the face.

## Four colors

This breed has four coat colors—tricolor, blenheim, black-and-tan, and ruby. The blenheim variety sometimes has a thumb-shaped mark on top of its head known as the "Blenheim spot."

Four coat colors

King Charles II loved his Spaniels so much that he made sure they were allowed everywhere, even inside the Houses of Parliament.

This breed has a furry tail.

79

# Doggie delights

A healthy diet is important for dogs. Owners should pick different dog foods, but introduce new ones gradually, and always put out fresh water. Dogs eat dry complete food, wet complete food, or a mix of both food types.

## Diet for growing pups

Pups should only eat puppy food, because it's softer than adult food and needs less chewing. This helps their smaller mouths and growing teeth. Puppy food has more protein, calcium, and fat to help tooth and bone growth.

## Wet food

This type of food smells strongly, so dogs love it. It is easy to swallow, and keeps dogs hydrated.

## Sweet snack

Dry doggie biscuits can be given as a reward to dogs for good behavior every now and then. But they shouldn't be overfed with these snacks.

## Dry food

A good quality dry food is packed with nutrients. Dry food can be left out in a bowl all day for the dog to eat.

*Since dry food needs to be chewed well, it keeps a dog's teeth healthy.*

*Mini marrowbone rolls*

## Best treats

Mini marrowbone rolls are the perfect treat for dogs. Packed with vitamins, minerals, and calcium, they keep a dog healthy and happy.

## What not to eat

It may be a treat for humans, but chocolate is dangerous and even deadly to dogs. Some of the other foods dogs can't eat are onions, grapes, garlic, nuts, and raisins.

Onion

Garlic

Raisins

Chocolate

Grapes

Nuts

## Water

A bowl of fresh, clean water should be kept out for dogs. Wet food also contains some water.

# Crossbreeds

A dog whose parents are of two different known breeds is called a crossbreed. It may inherit some of the physical features and personality of its parents. The name of a crossbreed usually includes parts from the names of both parents.

A dog with more than two breeds in its family is called a mixed breed, or mutt.

The Lurcher's neck is long and muscular.

## Fact file
- » **Origin:** United Kingdom
- » **Height:** 22–28 in (55–71 cm)
- » **Color:** Variety of colors
- » **Character:** Responsive, quiet, and active

## Lurcher
A natural racer, this dog is a cross between the Greyhound and the Collie or Terrier. The Lurcher combines the speed of the Greyhound with the enthusiasm of the Collie.

## Fact file
- » **Origin:** United Kingdom
- » **Height:** 9–12 in (23–30 cm)
- » **Color:** White; light tan
- » **Character:** Smart, friendly, and well-behaved

## Lucas Terrier
The Lucas Terrier is a mix of the Norfolk Terrier and the Sealyham Terrier. Like most terriers, this dog loves to play and dig.

The Lucas Terrier has a bushy moustache and beard.

## Fact file

- » **Origin:** United States
- » **Height:** Up to 24 in (61 cm)
- » **Color:** Variety of colors
- » **Character:** Energetic, gentle, and sociable

# Goldendoodle

A mix of the Golden Retriever and the Poodle, this dog is easy to train and gets along well with children. It can be an excellent guide and therapy dog, like its Retriever parent.

The Goldendoodle's coat is thick and curly.

The Labradinger has amber-colored eyes.

## Fact file

- » **Origin:** United States
- » **Height:** 18–22 in (46–56 cm)
- » **Color:** Yellow; liver; chocolate
- » **Character:** Lively, energetic, and affectionate

# Labradinger

Also called the Springador, this breed is a cross between the Labrador and the English Springer Spaniel. Like its parent breeds, the Labradinger is an active dog that needs a lot of exercise.

## Fact file

- » **Origin:** United States
- » **Height:** Toy: Up to 10 in (Up to 25 cm);
  Miniature: 11–14 in (28–35 cm);
  Standard: Over 15 in (Over 38 cm)
- » **Color:** Variety of colors
- » **Character:** Smart, social, and calm

The Cockapoo's droopy ears are covered with long, silky hair.

# Cockapoo

The Cockapoo has the Miniature or Toy Poodle and the American or English Cocker Spaniel for parents. This dog gets its friendliness from the Cocker Spaniel and is easy to train, like the Poodle.

# Labradoodle

This dog's name is a combination of its parents' names—Labrador and Poodle. The Labradoodle has the energy of a Labrador and the intelligence of a Poodle.

**Fact file**

» **Origin:** Australia
» **Height:** Miniature:
   14–16 in (36–41 cm);
   Medium: 17–20 in
   (43–51 cm); Standard:
   21–24 in (53–61 cm)
» **Color:** Variety of colors
» **Character:** Fun-loving,
   affectionate, and smart

The Labradoodle has large, round eyes.

Its coat can be wavy or curly.

The Labradoodle is a good breed for people with dog allergies, since it does not shed a lot.

Children having fun with a Labradoodle

## Bringing joy
The Labradoodle gets along well with children, and can be a gentle and loving companion. It is often chosen as a therapy dog for children, to help them feel calm and happy.

The tail is long and curled.

# Chiweenie

A cross between the Chihuahua and Dachshund, the Chiweenie is a great watchdog. This small dog has the long body of a Dachshund and the enthusiasm of a Chihuahua.

» **Origin:** North America
» **Height:** 6–10 in (15–25 cm)
» **Color:** Variety of colors
» **Character:** Friendly, active, playful, and loving

This dog was once called the "Mexican hotdog."

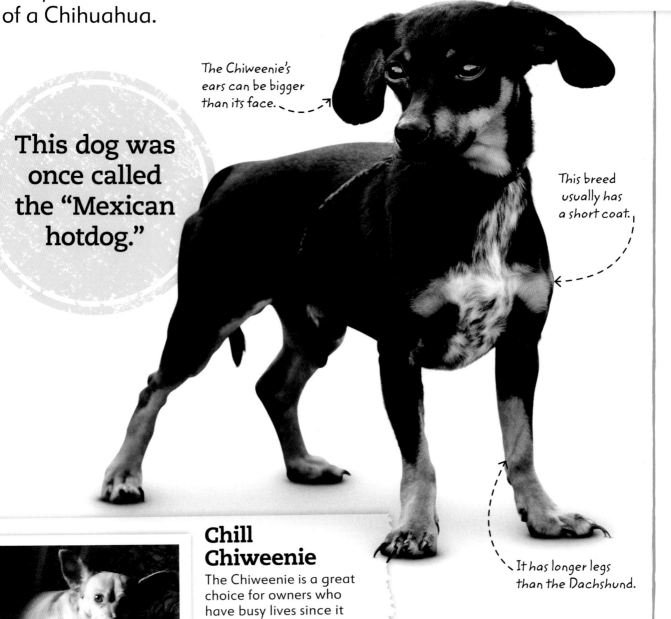

The Chiweenie's ears can be bigger than its face.

This breed usually has a short coat.

It has longer legs than the Dachshund.

## Chill Chiweenie

The Chiweenie is a great choice for owners who have busy lives since it requires less grooming. This dog settles well in small apartments.

Chiweenie at home

# Training

A pet needs to be trained from a young age in order to learn new behaviors. At first, the basics need to be covered to ensure the dog understands and responds to these simple commands. Dog treats work well as a reward.

### "Come"

The dog should be trained to come when called, without getting distracted. A treat can be used to encourage the pooch to follow the instruction.

_The dog must know this command if it is allowed off the leash._

### "Walk"

This soon becomes a favorite word with dogs, and they never forget it! Calm behaviour is often rewarded when the command is said, and when dogs do not pull while walking.

### "Stay"

The dog is trained to rest in a position until a further command is given. This is best taught when the dog is tired and willing to relax.

Adult dogs are better at learning tricks since they have better focus.

## "Sit"

Getting a dog to sit on command can be useful to keep it still, for example, when waiting to cross the road at traffic lights. This is one of the easiest commands for a dog to learn.

## Toilet training

It is important to toilet train puppies from a young age. This can begin inside, by taking the pup to a pee pad or newspaper after meals and naps. Over time, the pup can be taken outside regularly to build a routine.

## "Leave it!"

This command is handy when a dog is required to immediately stop doing an action. A firm "Leave it!" instruction might be useful if there is a lot of food around, and a hungry dog!

## "No!"

If a dog misbehaves, a strong "No!" helps to reprimand it. But if the dog makes a mistake or does not follow a command, it's best that the owners do not to get angry—as this might make the dog nervous.

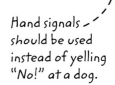

Hand signals should be used instead of yelling "No!" at a dog.

# Playtime

Dogs are very intelligent, and play allows them to learn and have fun. It is particularly important for puppies as they begin to understand how to behave. Playing with a dog is also a great way to bond and reinforce training.

Playing together allows the puppies to make friends with one another. It helps them learn how to communicate with each other.

Play helps dogs get rid of bad habits, such as excessive chewing.

Play sessions should be kept short to avoid the puppy from getting worn out. Having a variety of games helps the dog to not get bored.

## Types of game

Pooch games are best played with dog toys, since they are safe and dog-friendly. The main rule is that the dog must leave the toy when asked to. Here are some games they love to play.

### Fetch

Chasing a ball and bringing it back to its owner lets a dog burn off energy. It also helps a dog to learn to come back when called.

### Tug-of-war

Special tug toys can be used for this game. It can be made more challenging by giving the dog fewer chances to win.

### Hide-and-seek

Dogs love to sniff out and find their favorite things—including their owners! The owner can ask the dog to sit or stay and then hide for it to find them.

# All together

This book shows off just some of the many dog breeds that exist today. Here you'll find a selection of the breeds shown in the book.

**Black Russian Terrier**
pg. 16

**Irish Terrier**
pg. 16

**Boston Terrier**
pg. 17

**Fox Terrier**
pg. 17

**Affenpinscher**
pg. 17

**Airedale Terrier**
pg. 18

**Jack Russell Terrier**
pg. 19

**West Highland White Terrier**
pg. 20

**Yorkshire Terrier**
pg. 21

**Scottish Terrier**
pg. 22

**Border Terrier**
pg. 23

**Basset Hound**
pg. 28

**Bruno Jura**
pg. 28

**Finnish Hound**
pg. 29

**Sloughi**
pg. 29

**Pharaoh Hound**
pg. 29

**Norwegian Elkhound**
pg. 30

**Miniature Dachshund**
pg. 31

**Afghan Hound**
pg. 32

**Greyhound**
pg. 33

**Beagle**
pg. 34

**Bloodhound**
pg. 35

**Irish Setter**
pg. 38

**English Setter**
pg. 38

**Labrador Retriever**
pg. 39

**American Water Spaniel**
pg. 39

**German Spaniel**
pg. 39

**Weimaraner**
pg. 40

**Golden Retriever**
pg. 41

**American Cocker Spaniel**
pg. 42

**English Springer Spaniel**
pg. 43

**Chesapeake Bay Retriever**
pg. 44

**Brittany**
pg. 45

**Italian Spinone**
pg. 46

**Blue Picardy Spaniel**
pg. 47

**Czechoslovakian Wolfdog**
pg. 48

**Dutch Shepherd**
pg. 48

**Neapolitan Mastiff**
pg. 49

**Pyrenean Mountain Dog** pg. 49

 **Saint Bernard** pg. 50

 **Siberian Husky** pg. 51

 **Komondor** pg. 52

 **Bernese Mountain Dog** pg. 53

 **Briard** pg. 54

 **Boxer** pg. 55

 **Newfoundland** pg. 56

 **Great Dane** pg. 57

 **Icelandic Sheepdog** pg. 60

 **Entlebucher Mountain Dog** pg. 60

 **Groenendael** pg. 61

 **Australian Shepherd** pg. 61

 **Belgian Tervuren** pg. 61

 **Pembroke Welsh Corgi** pg. 62

 **Old English Sheepdog** pg. 63

 **Border Collie** pg. 64

 **German Shepherd** pg. 65

 **Keeshond** pg. 66

 **Chinese Shar-Pei** pg. 67

 **Norwegian Lundehund** pg. 67

 **Löwchen** pg. 67

 **Dalmatian** pg. 68

 **Poodle** pg. 69

 **Chow Chow** pg. 70

 **Shiba Inu** pg. 71

 **Shih Tzu** pg. 72

 **Japanese Chin** pg. 72

 **Papillon** pg. 73

 **Pomeranian** pg. 73

 **Chihuahua** pg. 73

 **Chinese Crested Dog** pg. 74

 **French Bulldog** pg. 75

 **Pekingese** pg. 76

 **Pug** pg. 77

 **Bichon Frise** pg. 78

 **Cavalier King Charles Spaniel** pg. 79

 **Lurcher** pg. 82

 **Lucas Terrier** pg. 82

 **Goldendoodle** pg. 83

 **Labradinger** pg. 83

 **Cockapoo** pg. 83

 **Labradoodle** pg. 84

 **Chiweenie** pg. 85

# Glossary

**agile**

ability to move quickly and easily, with grace

**allergy**

bad reaction to fur or another substance, which usually brings on watery eyes and sneezing

**ancestor**

animal related to another, more recent animal. The wolf is the ancestor of the dog

**breed**

type of animal with specific characteristics

**burrow**

to dig into the ground

**cancer**

disease in which cells begin to grow uncontrollably, causing harm to the body

**canine**

relating to dogs

**cattle**

farm animals from the Bovidae family, such as cows and buffaloes

**coat**

fur or hair on an animal's body

**command**

to give an order or instruction

**companion**

friend, or someone you spend a lot of time with

**corded**

coat type in which fur develops into long, thick cords. The Komondor has a corded coat

**crossbreed**

dog whose parents are of two different known breeds

**dense**

something that is tightly packed together, for example, hair

**disability**

medical condition that restricts an individual's movement

**expedition**

long journey undertaken for a purpose, such as exploration

**groom**

to brush and clean fur, or to cut nails or hair

**harness**

set of straps that can be secured around a dog's body and attached to a leash for better control

**hospice**

hospital for dying people, or a shelter for travelers, especially one kept by monks

**howl**

long, loud sound made by wolves and dogs

**hygiene**

practice of keeping oneself and one's surroundings clean

**instinct**

way of behaving, thinking, or feeling that comes naturally

**leash**

(also called lead) long, thin strap that can be secured to a dog's collar or harness during walks, or to keep the dog nearby

**litter**

all the puppies that are born to a mother at the same time

**livestock**

animals that are kept on farms, including cows, sheep, goats, and pigs

**marmoset**

small monkey from South and Central America that has large eyes, thick fur, and a long tail covered in hair

**marshland**

low-lying land that stays wet and muddy all year round

**mat**

hair or fur tangled into a thick lump

**medical sample**

(also called specimen) small portion of an individual's blood, body fluid, or body tissue that is examined in a laboratory to look for sickness or disease

**muzzle**

part of a dog's face that usually includes its nose and mouth

**nutrients**

different substances needed to maintain health, growth, and development

**pitch**

highness or lowness of a sound

**posture**

position of the body when standing, sitting, or walking

**retrieve**

to find and bring back something

**scent**

smell that a person, animal or substance gives off. Some dogs are very good at following scents

**sheepdog trial**

competition in which the skills of herding dogs are tested and displayed

**sled**

vehicle used to travel on snow

**snipe**

bird with a long, straight beak that lives in wet areas

**snowstorm**

heavy snowfall accompanied by strong winds

**terrain**

type of land, such as hilly or flat

**therapy**

form of treatment designed to improve the well-being of people

**topcoat**

coat of heavy hair. In dogs with two coats, topcoat hairs grow past undercoat hairs

**track**

to find and chase an animal or person

**undercoat**

thick, usually short, soft coat. In dogs with two coats, undercoat hairs are shorter than topcoat hairs

**vermin**

small animal pests, including rodents and foxes

**vet**

(also called veterinarian) someone who treats and operates on injured or sick animals

**visually impaired**

someone who cannot see, partially or fully

**wading bird**

long-legged bird that walks in water to grab fish, insects, or frogs

**watchdog**

dog that guards someone's property

**waterfowl**

birds that swim in water, including ducks and geese

**waterproof**

something that does not let water pass through it. Many dogs have a waterproof coat

**wean**

process by which young puppies are encouraged to feed on food other than their mother's milk

**webbed**

when there is excess skin between the toes, resembling a duck's foot

# Index

## A

Affenpinscher 17
Afghan Hound 7, 32
Airedale Terrier 18
allergy-detection dogs 58
American Cocker Spaniel 42
American Hairless Terrier 7
American Water Spaniel 39
ancestors 5
anger 37
army dogs 59
Australian Shepherd 61

## B

bad habits 89
balance 5
barking 36–37
Basset Hound 28
bathing 10
Beagle 34
beds 9
Belgian Tervuren 61
Bernese Mountain Dog 53
Bichon Frise 7, 78
birds, finding/catching 38
biscuits 81
Black Russian Terrier 16
Bloodhound 35
Blue Picardy Spaniel 47
body language 5
body structure 4–5
Bolognese 78
bombs, detecting 59
bones 4
Border Collie 64
Border Terrier 23
Boston Terrier 17
Boxer 6, 55
Briard 54
Brittany 45
Bruno Jura 28
brushes 11

## C

canine group 4
Cavalier King Charles Spaniel 79

Charles II, King 79
Chesapeake Bay Retriever 44
Chihuahua 5, 73
Chinese Crested Dog 7, 74
Chinese Shar-Pei 66–67
Chiweenie 85
Chow Chow 6, 70
claws 5, 11
coats 4, 6–7, 10–11
Cockapoo 83
collars 8
color varieties 6–7
combs 11
"come" command 86
commands 13, 86–87
communication 5, 26–27, 36–37
crates 9
crossbreeds 82–83, 84–85
curly coats 7, 11
Czechoslovakian Wolfdog 48

## D

Dachshund 31
Dalmatian 6, 68
defensiveness 27
detection dogs 59
diet 80–81
digging 16, 20
disabilities, people with 58–59
diseases, detecting 58
double coats 6
drugs, detecting 59
dry food 80, 81
Dutch Shepherd 48

## E

ears 4, 11, 24, 25
Elizabeth II, Queen 62
emotions 26, 27
English Setter 38
English Springer Spaniel 43
Entlebucher Mountain Dog 60
excitement 27
exploring 14
eyes 4, 5, 12, 24

## F

fear 27, 37
feeding 8, 12, 13, 15, 80–81
fetch game 89

fighting 13, 15, 25
films, dogs in 21, 23, 49, 65
Finnish Hound 29
fire-station dogs 68
flat-faced dogs 76–77
Fox Terrier 17
foxes 4, 36
French Bulldog 75

## G

games 9, 89
German Shepherd 65
German Spaniel 39
Giant Schnauzer 6
Golden Retriever 41
Goldendoodle 41, 83
Great Dane 5, 57
Greyhound 6, 33
Groenendael 61
grooming 8, 10–11, 36
growling 37
guard dogs 4, 48, 54, 59
guide dogs 58

## H

hairless dogs 7
hairstyles 69
harnesses 8
hearing 4, 24
hearing dogs 59
herding dogs 4, 48, 60–61, 62–65
hero dogs 59
hide-and-seek 89
hounds 28–29, 30–35
howling 5, 36
hunting 4, 57
hygiene 11

## I

Icelandic Sheepdog 60
Irish Setter 38
Irish Terrier 16
Italian Spinone 46

## J

Jack Russell Terrier 19
jackals 4
Japanese Chin 72

Jefferson, Thomas 54
jobs 48, 58–59

## K

Keeshond 66
Komondor 52

## L

Labradinger 83
Labradoodle 7, 84
Labrador Retriever 6, 39
lap warmers 75
leashes 8
"leave it" command 87
legs 5
litters 12
loads, pulling 48, 53
long coat 7, 10
Löwchen 67
Lucas Terrier 82
Lurcher 82

## M

meat 80
medical-alert-and-detection dogs 58
milk 10
mines, detecting 59
mixed breeds 82
mobility-assistance dogs 59
mutts 82

## N

nails 11
Neapolitan Mastiff 49
Newfoundland 56
"no" command 87
nonsporting dogs 66–67, 68–71
Norwegian Elkhound 30
Norwegian Lundehund 66–67
nursing 12

## O

obedience 86–87
Old English Sheepdog 63

## P

Papillon 73
paws 5
Pekingese 76
Pembroke Welsh Corgi 62
petting 15
Pharaoh Hound 29

pitch, barking 37
play 14, 15, 88–89
play-fighting 13
police dogs 35, 55
Pomeranian 73
Poodle 7, 69
pregnancy 12
Pug 77
Puli 52
puppies 12–15, 88–89
Pyrenean Mountain Dog 49

## R

rescue dogs 48, 50, 59
routine 9, 15
running 5

## S

Saint Bernard 50
scent hounds 28
scissors 11
Scottish Terrier 22
senses 4, 5, 12, 13, 24–25
shampoo 11
Shiba Inu 71
Shih Tzu 72
short coats 6, 10
Siberian Husky 51
sight 4, 5, 24
sight hounds 28
"sit" command 87
size 5
sled dogs 51
sleep 9, 12
Sloughi 29
smell, sense of 5, 13, 25, 38, 69
snacks 81
socialization 14, 88
speed 64
sporting dogs 38–39, 40–47
"stay" command 86
swimming 56

## T

tails 5, 26–27
taste, sense of 4, 25
teeth cleaning 11
terriers 16–17, 18–23
toilet training 87
tongues 4, 55, 70
topcoat hairs 6
touch, sense of 25
toy dogs 72–73, 74–79
toys 9, 89
training 13, 14–15, 58, 86–87, 88
treats 9, 11, 81, 86
truffle-hunting 69
tug-of-war 89

## U

undercoat hairs 6

## V

vets 11

## W

wagging tails 26–27
"walk" command 86
walks 9, 86
warnings 37
water 8, 9, 81
weaning 13
Weimaraner 40
West Highland White Terrier 20
wet food 80
wire-haired coats 6, 11
wolves 4, 5
working dogs 48–49, 50–59

## Y

yapping 36–37
yelping 36, 37
Yorkshire Terrier 21

# Acknowledgments

Dorling Kindersley would like to thank Radhika Haswani for editorial assistance, Polly Goodman for proofreading, and Helen Peters for the index.

**The publisher would like to thank the following for their kind permission to reproduce their photographs:**

(Key: a-above; b-below/bottom; c-center; f-far; l-left; r-right; t-top)

1 Dreamstime.com: Erik Lam (c). 1–96 Dreamstime.com: Willeecole (background). 2 Dreamstime.com: Ksena2009 (tc); Peter Zijlstra (ca); Ljupco (bc). 3 123RF.com: Elnur Amikishiyev (tl). Dreamstime.com: Chernetskaya (tr); Nadisja (tc); Akaphat Porntepkasemsan (bc); Jagodka (br); Gveter2 (crb); Jaroslav Frank (fbr). 4–5 Dreamstime.com: Tomislav Birtic. 5 Alamy Stock Photo: Elles Rijsdijk (tc). Dreamstime.com: LazyFocus (cra); Otsphoto (ca); Maryswift (cr); Starzon450 (crb). 6 Dreamstime.com: Jagodka (cl); Tandemich (c); Erik Lam (cr). 7 Dreamstime.com: Nynke Van Holten (c); Jagodka (cl); Erik Lam (cr). 8 123RF.com: Elnur Amikishiyev (cr). Dreamstime.com: Chernetskaya (tr); Karenr (cl); Nadisja (bl). 9 Dreamstime.com: Ksena2009 (cl); Vadim Usov (tl); Weerapat Wattanapichayakul (c); Peter Zijlstra (c/Dog toys, clb); Ljupco (br); Photodeti (br). 10 Dreamstime.com: Roughcollie (cl); Vadym Soloviov (cr). 11 Dreamstime.com: Chernetskaya (bc); Gveter2 (fcla); Jaroslav Frank (ca); Akaphat Porntepkasemsan (tc); Elena Yakimova (cr); Forestpath (cl); Onepony (cl). Getty Images / iStock: undefined undefined (cra). 12 Dreamstime.com: Zuzana Uhlkov (cl). 13 Dreamstime.com: Erik Lam (c). 14–15 Dreamstime.com: Daniel Budiman (t). 14 Alamy Stock Photo: blickwinkel / Schmidt-Roeger (bc). 15 Dreamstime.com: Denis Moskvinov (cl). Getty Images / iStock: BraunS / E+ (bl). 16 Alamy Stock Photo: MilanStock.com (bl). Dreamstime.com: Isselee (tr). 17 Dorling Kindersley: A.J. Teasdale (bc). 18 Alamy Stock Photo: Chronicle (cl). 20 Alamy Stock Photo: Duncan Astbury (bc). Dreamstime.com: Isselee (c). 21 Alamy Stock Photo: Pictorial Press Ltd (cr). Dreamstime.com: Sergey Lavrentev / Laures (cra). 22 Alamy Stock Photo: Classic Image (cra); James Talalay (cla). 23 Alamy Stock Photo: Moviestore Collection Ltd (crb). Dreamstime.com: Isselee (bb). 24 Dreamstime.com: Maryswift (cl). Getty Images / iStock: malamooshi (bc). 25 Dreamstime.com: Lars Christnsen (bc/Ears pulled back); Isselee (tl, bc); Willeecole (cl); Lensonfocus (cr). Getty Images / iStock: Lyly / E+ (cr). 26–27 Getty Images / iStock: Upyanose. 27 Dorling Kindersley: Berry (cr). 28 Dorling Kindersley: P.Guenole (br). Dreamstime.com: Luckynick (cr). 29 Dorling Kindersley: T.Olkkonen; A.Vilpula (tl). Dreamstime.com: Willeecole (b). naturepl.com: Petra Wegner (cr). 30 Alamy Stock Photo: Everett Collection Inc (br). 31 Dreamstime.com: Cynoclub (br); Jagodka (cl); Willeecole (bc). 32 Dreamstime.com: Maria Itina (bl); Trapeza (r). Getty Images: Bettmann (cl). 33 Alamy Stock Photo: Julie Mowbray (c). Dreamstime.com: Spiroview Inc. (c). 34 Alamy Stock Photo: Molika An (cr). Dreamstime.com: Chalermphon Kumchai (c). 35 Alamy Stock Photo: dpa picture alliance (cr). Dorling Kindersley: Richards (c). 36–37 Dreamstime.com: Irina Nedikova. 36 Dreamstime.com: Adogslifephoto (cr); Cynoclub (bc); Isselee (cra, br). 37 Dorling Kindersley: Grimsdell (bl). Dreamstime.com: Isselee (tr). 39 Dorling Kindersley: L.Ahlsson (b). 40 Dreamstime.com: Farinoza (r). 41 Dreamstime.com: Jeroen Van Den Broek (bc); Andrey Pavlov (c). 42 Dreamstime.com: Isselee (c); Zuzana Tillerov (cr). 43 Alamy Stock Photo:

Masterpics (bc). 44 Alamy Stock Photo: Bob Langrish (c). Marlayna Demond for UMBC: (br). 45 Alamy Stock Photo: Perky Pets (cl). Dreamstime.com: BarbaraCerovsek (cr); Cgracer (crb). 46 Alamy Stock Photo: Nature Picture Library (c); The Print Collector (cra). Dreamstime.com: Zuzana Tillerov (bc). 47 Alamy Stock Photo: Imagebroker (bl). 48–49 Dreamstime.com: Cynoclub (ca). 48 Dreamstime.com: Miraswonderland (b). 49 Dreamstime.com: Cynoclub (bl). 50 Alamy Stock Photo: KGPA Ltd (clb). 51 Carrie M. McLain Memorial Museum: (cr). 52 Dreamstime.com: Photographerlondon (c); Szabolcs Stieber (bc). 53 Dreamstime.com: Slowmotiongli (cla). 54 Dreamstime.com: Isselee (c); Richie Lomba (crb). 55 Dreamstime.com: Gloria Anderson (c); Isselee (l). 56 123RF.com: Eric Isselee (br). Alamy Stock Photo: IanDagnall Computing (bl); Grossemy Vanessa (c). 57 Dreamstime.com: Isselee (b); Aleksandr Zotov (cl). 58 Alamy Stock Photo: rfranca (cl). Dreamstime.com: Roman Chazov (cra). Medical Detection Dogs: Neil Pollock (br). 59 Alamy Stock Photo: Arterra Picture Library (cla). Dreamstime.com: Chernetskaya (cra). Getty Images / iStock: casiano (br); Philartphace (cr); gollykim (bl). 60 Dreamstime.com: Erik Lam (tr); Igor Marx (bc). 60–61 Dreamstime.com: Isselee (bc). 61 Dreamstime.com: Isselee (tl, cra). 62 Dreamstime.com: Camptoloma (cr). Getty Images: Anwar Hussein (bl). 63 Alamy Stock Photo: Stefan Rousseau / PA Images (cr); eriklam / YAY Media AS (fcra). 64 Dreamstime.com: Isselee (b). Getty Images / iStock: Markanja (cla). 65 Alamy Stock Photo: Album (cra). Getty Images / iStock: alvarez / E+ (cla). 66 Dreamstime.com: Isselee (bc). 66–67 Dreamstime.com: Isselee (b). 67 Alamy Stock Photo: Perky Pets (crb). 68 Dreamstime.com: Farinoza (b). Getty Images / iStock: Mehmet Hilmi Barcin (cra). Getty Images: Richard Hutchings (cl). 69 Dreamstime.com: Jagodka (bl); Ruibo Wang (c). 70 Dreamstime.com: Lilun (b). Getty Images: Sigmund Freud Copyrights / ullstein bild (cla). 71 Dreamstime.com: Darkkong (bl); Andrey Yakovlev (b). 72 Dreamstime.com: Jagodka (cr); Dmitri Pravdjukov (bc). 73 Dreamstime.com: Isselee (bb); Trapeza (b). 74 Dreamstime.com: Isselee (cl); Andrey Medvedev (b). 75 Alamy Stock Photo: www.picturethepast.org.uk / Nottingham City Council / Heritage Images (cra). Dreamstime.com: Erik Lam (b). 76 Alamy Stock Photo: Paul Fearn (br). Dreamstime.com: Jagodka (c). 77 Alamy Stock Photo: Amoret Tanner (crb). Dreamstime.com: Viorel Sima (bl). 78 Alamy Stock Photo: Imagebroker (cla); Rainer Lesniewski (cra). Dreamstime.com: Isselee (b). 79 Alamy Stock Photo: Grossemy Vanessa (crb). 80 Dreamstime.com: Chernetskaya (crb); Willeecole (cl); Richard Nelson (cr). 81 Dreamstime.com: Exopixel (bc); Sarah Marchant (tl); Nevinates (tr, crb); Johnfoto (cra/Garlic); Ionutv91 (cra); Philip Kinsey (cb). 82 Dorling Kindersley: Tracy Morgan: C.Labers (cl). 83 Dreamstime.com: David Calvert (tr); Erik Lam (br). 84 Dreamstime.com: Nynke Van Holten (br). Getty Images: LWA / Stone (cr). 85 Dreamstime.com: William Wise (b). Getty Images / iStock: Katherine Joseph (bl). 86 Alamy Stock Photo: Dorling Kindersley ltd (cl). Dreamstime.com: Sergiy Bykhunenko (cr); Alexey Maximenko (bl). 87 Alamy Stock Photo: Pixel-shot (tr). Dreamstime.com: Natalia Fomina (cl); Isselee (tl); Willeecole (bc, crb). 88–89 Alamy Stock Photo: Cavan Images. 89 Dreamstime.com: Alexey Maximenko (crb);

Mdorottya (cra); Roughcollie (br). 90 Alamy Stock Photo: Bob Langrish (bl/Brown); MilanStock.com (cla/Orange); Julie Mowbray (c); Perky Pets (bl); Nature Picture Library (bc/Roan). Dorling Kindersley: T.Olkkonen; A.Vilpula (cra/Hound); A.J. Teasdale (ca/Black); P.Guenole (ca); Richards (cr); Grimsdell (fclb); L.A. & B.Williams (clb/Hound); L.Ahlsson (cb). Dreamstime.com: Cynoclub (br/Wolf); Sergey Lavrentev / Laures (fcla); Isselee (fcla/Black, cla, fcra/White, fcr, fcrb); Luckynick (ca/Hound); Willeecole (fcra); Jagodka (cl/Black); Trapeza (cl); Chalermphon Kumchai (cr/Beagle); Farinoza (crb/Grey); Andrey Pavlov (crb); Miraswonderland (br). 91 123RF.com: Nynke van Holten (bl); Eric Isselee (ftr). Alamy Stock Photo: Perky Pets (bc); eriklam (cra/Old). Dorling Kindersley: Tracy Morgan: C.Labers (crb). Dreamstime.com: David Calvert (fcrb); Cynoclub (ftl); Isselee (tl, tr/Briard, tr, ca/Black, ca/Belgian, cra/Australian, cla, ca, cr, cb/White, cb); Photographerlondon (tc/White); Erik Lam (cla/Spitz, fclb, bl/Brown); Igor Marx (cla/Mountain); Camptoloma (cra/Corgi); Farinoza (cra/Dalmatian); Ruibo Wang (fcra); Lilun (fcl); Andrey Yakovlev (cl/Inu); Jagodka (cl, clb/Orange); Dmitri Pravdjukov (c/Chin); Trapeza (c); Andrey Medvedev (fcr); Viorel Sima (clb); William Wise (b). Getty Images / iStock: alvarez / E+ (cla/German); GlobalP (fcla/Dane). 92 Alamy Stock Photo: Elles Rijsdijk (br). Dreamstime.com: Karenr (tr). 93 Dreamstime.com: Chalermphon Kumchai (br). 94 Dreamstime.com: Cynoclub (tr); Weerapat Wattanapichayakul (bl); Willeecole (tc); Jagodka (ftr). 95 Dreamstime.com: Jagodka (br). 96 Dreamstime.com: Camptoloma (br).

Cover images: Front: 123RF.com: Elnur Amikishiyev (cr); Dreamstime.com: David Calvert (ftr), Isselee (crb), Jagodka (cl), Erik Lam bl, Sergey Lavrentev / Laures (cla), Alexey Maximenko (bc), Peter Zijlstra (ftl); Fotolia: Paul Cotney (br), Eric Isselee (tr); Back: Alamy Stock Photo: Nature Picture Library (bl)/(Italian Spinone dog); Dorling Kindersley: L.A. & B.Williams (tc); Dreamstime.com: Camptoloma (cl), Isselee (clb, cr, bl, cb), Dmitri Pravdjukov (crb), Trapeza (bc); Spine: Dreamstime.com: Isselee (t), Trapeza (b).

All other images © Dorling Kindersley